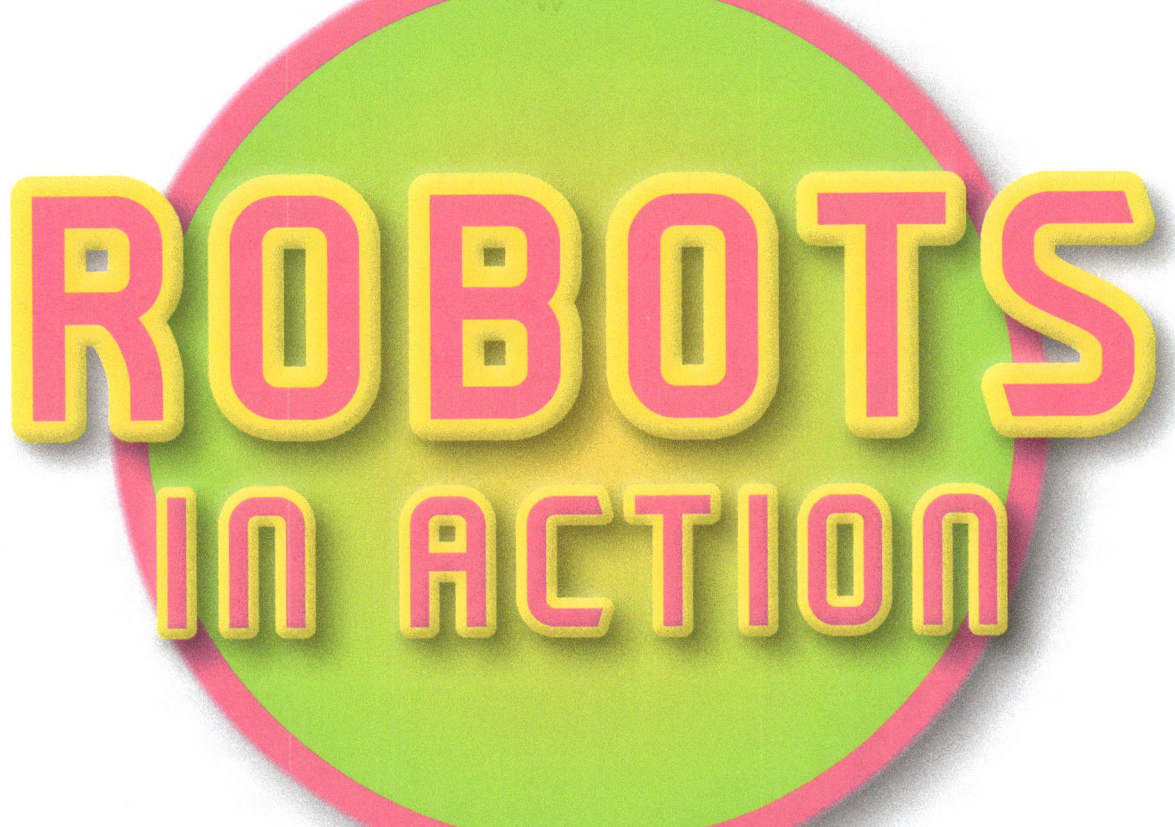

www.worldbook.com

Co-published by agreement between Shi Tu Hui and World Book, Inc.

Shi Tu Hui
Room 1807, Block 1,
#3 West Dawang Road
Chaoyang District, Beijing 100025
P.R. China

World Book, Inc.
180 North LaSalle Street
Suite 900
Chicago, Illinois 60601
USA

© 2026. All rights reserved. This volume may not be reproduced in whole or in part in any form without prior written permission from the publisher.

WORLD BOOK and the GLOBE DEVICE are registered trademarks or trademarks of World Book, Inc.

Library of Congress Control Number: 2025938163

Robots
ISBN: 978-0-7166-5814-6 (set, hard cover)

Robots in Action
ISBN: 978-0-7166-5821-4 (hard cover)

Also available as:
ISBN: 978-0-7166-5831-3 (soft cover)
ISBN: 978-0-7166-5841-2 (e-book)

WORLD BOOK STAFF

Writer: William D. Adams

Editorial

Vice President
Tom Evans

Senior Manager, New Content
Jeff De La Rosa

Associate Manager, New Content
William D. Adams

Content Creator
Elizabeth Huyck

Proofreader
Nathalie Strassheim

Graphics and Design

Senior Visual Communications Designer
Melanie Bender

Photo Editor
Rosalia Bledsoe

ACKNOWLEDGMENTS

Cover: © 35lab/Shutterstock; © Science Photo Library/Alamy Images; © Carlos Sanchez, Texas A&M University; © Dean John Kd De Dios, US Army
4-5 © Perfect Gui/Shutterstock; © Press Lab/Shutterstock; © Walter Myers, Science Source
6-7 Monika Hess, U.S. Navy; © Raj Valley, Alamy Images
8-9 Kenji Thuloweit, U.S. Air Force
10-11 Rhita Daniel, U.S. Marine Corps
12-13 Leslie Pratt, U.S. Air Force; Neil Ballecer, Air National Guard
14-15 © Joshua Hoskins, Air Force; © Chesky/Shutterstock
16-17 © Milrem AS
18-19 © Dean John Kd De Dios, US Army; © Digital Storm/Shutterstock
20-21 Jodi Ames, U.S. Air Force; Jeremy L. Wood, U.S. Navy
22-23 Department of Defense
24-25 © Shuji Kajiyama, AP Photo
26-27 NASA; University of Nevada, Las Vegas
28-29 © Carlos Sanchez, Texas A&M University; © Eric Whitmire, North Carolina State University
30-31 © Aurelien Meunier, Getty Images
32-33 © RoboCup Federation
34-35 NASA/JPL-Caltech
36-37 NASA
38-39 NASA/Johns Hopkins University Applied Physics Laboratory/Southwest Research Institute; NASA/JPL-Caltech
40-41 CNSA
42-43 © Science Photo Library/Alamy Images; NASA/JPL-Caltech/ASU/MSSS
44-45 © Carnegie Mellon University
46-47 © Cristian Cristel, Xinhua/Getty Images

Contents

- 4 Introduction
- 6 Robots in the Military
- 8 In the Loop
- 10 Military Drone Aircraft
- 12 HELLO, MY NAME IS: MQ-9 Reaper
- 14 Swarming Aircraft
- 16 Military Ground Vehicles
- 18 ROBOT RISK: Ethics of Military Robots
- 20 Bomb Disposal Units
- 22 Robots in Disasters
- 24 HELLO, MY NAME IS: Little Sunfish
- 26 Types of Rescue Robots
- 28 HELLO, MY NAME IS: Cyborg rescue cockroach
- 30 Firefighting Robots
- 32 RoboCup Rescue Robot League
- 34 Robots in Space Exploration
- 36 HELLO, MY NAME IS: Canadarm2
- 38 Space Probes
- 40 Landers and Rovers
- 42 HELLO, MY NAME IS: Perseverance
- 44 Other Extreme Environments
- 46 Hands-On Robotics
- 48 Glossary and Index

Terms defined in the glossary are in type **that looks like this** on their first appearance on any spread (two facing pages).

Introduction

Many jobs, such as bolting parts together, vacuuming floors, or moving merchandise, are quite dull. Robots have excelled at these jobs, allowing humans to do more interesting things. But other jobs are far from dull. In fact, many can be extremely dangerous. People need to be found and rescued during disasters. The far reaches of space are ripe for exploring, but we can't safely send astronauts. Battlefields are inherently dangerous, defined by the risk of injury and death.

The robotics revolution is in full swing. Space probes and rovers already explore distant planets. **Drones,** bomb disposal units, and other uncrewed vehicles are a common sight on battlefields and in disaster zones. Engineers are making these machines more capable—and more **autonomous**—than ever before.

In this book, you will read about robots facing danger in the outside world. You will learn about how they are designed and programmed to overcome such danger. Finally, you'll meet some of the robots that are facing danger to go on military missions, protect people, and make new discoveries.

Disaster zones, battlefields, and outer space are dangerous places for people. Robots have long helped us to explore space, but new models are venturing into hazardous environments here on Earth.

[5]

Robots in the Military

For thousands of years, humans have used new technology to protect themselves, spy on their enemies, and make their weapons deadlier. Today, governments around the world are putting recent advances in **automation, artificial intelligence,** and robotics to work in strengthening their militaries.

A guided missile is a kind of robot. Some can fly and follow targets autonomously, though each can only be used once.

Sea sentinal
The Magura V5 from Ukraine is a fully autonomous sea drone that can patrol sea lanes, locate mines, carry torpedos, or swarm together to confound enemy ships.

As robots and software improve, more advanced **autonomous** robots are finding their way onto the battlefield. Fully autonomous guided missiles can sense the environment, locate a target, create a plan to hit the target, and act on the plan. In most combat situations a human still decides to launch the missile and chooses the target. But autonomous missiles and drones could be programmed to seek out and attack targets on their own. A human could fire the missile in a general direction, but the missile would pick a specific target. Robotic tanks, dogs, boats, and **humanoids** in the military are also gaining more autonomy.

[7]

In the Loop

In military situations, **automation** is managed through a *human-in-the-loop* decision-making process. In human-in-the-loop decision making, a robot or other machine performs a task and waits for a human operator to approve before performing the next task. Because this system requires a lot of human attention, some arms manufacturers are encouraging governments to accept *human-on-the-loop* decision-making for military robots. In human-on-the-loop decision making (also called supervised **autonomy**), a robot performs tasks continuously, but a human monitors its behavior and can stop the robot at any time. Rather than having one person closely monitor only one machine at a time, one person can supervise many robots. But this system raises a moral question. Is it acceptable for robots to fight costly wars while we merely supervise them? And will that change as robots get more intelligent?

[8]

A bomb disposal unit is often directed by remote control, so it will not take any action without a human command. This is example of a "human-in-the-loop" system.

Military Drone Aircraft

Modern militaries use many kinds of uncrewed aerial vehicles, also called **drones.** Drones are mainly used for surveillance. Some are tiny. They weigh little more than an ounce (30 grams). They are capable of scouting over hills or around corners to tell if it's safe for troops to move into those areas. Other military drones are large, with wingspans of 100 feet (30 meters) or more. They can fly to other countries to gather information.

Some drones are piloted remotely by a person on the ground. But many have greater **autonomy.** They can be programmed to gather information about an area, scan for people with infrared cameras, or spot artillery targets. Drones equipped with **artificial intelligence** can make their own decisions about where and how to fly to best achieve their goal and avoid danger.

Eye in the sky
U.S. Marines test a small reconnaissance drone. These drones help soldiers spot enemies before they can attack.

HELLO, MY NAME IS:

MQ-9 Reaper

The Reaper is an attack **drone** manufactured in the United States. It is too slow to avoid fighter jets or antiaircraft guns. But in areas where there are few such threats, the Reaper can be used to strike ground targets. It can fly around for a long time (called loitering), waiting for its target to come out into the open or move away from civilians. Reapers are taken apart and flown in large cargo planes to the places they are needed. Then, ground crews reassemble them and prepare them for flight.

AUTONOMY

LOW TO HIGH

The Reaper can be guided remotely by a human pilot, or it can be programmed to fly and seek out targets autonomously.

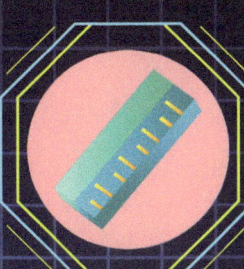

SIZE

36 feet (11 meters) long, 66-foot (20-meter) wingspan, 4,900 pounds (2,200 kilograms) when empty

TOP SPEED

About 276 miles (444 kilometers) per hour, slower than an average passenger airplane

MAKER

U.S. company General Atomics

Swarming Aircraft

When military units are in dangerous territory, it is essential to supply them with food, fuel, and ammunition. Truck convoys carrying goods are slow and at risk of enemy attack. They also deliver supplies in bulk, forcing soldiers to carry what they will need for the next several days. Instead, **autonomous drones** could be a better way to resupply armies in the field. Streams of drones could deliver smaller

Battle swarms
The autonomous Valkyrie drone can collect information, carry weapons, and pair with crewed aircraft. In combat, swarms of them can confuse enemy radar.

[14]

amounts of supplies more frequently. Troops could even order special equipment they need for a mission and have it delivered in minutes.

Swarms of autonomous aircraft are also being tested for aerial combat. These aircraft communicate with each other to evade enemies and choose targets. Larger crewed aircraft might not be able to destroy enough swarming drones before the drones bring them down.

During combat, figuring out who or what to attack is extremely important. Human fighters often rely on verbal communication. But robots could coordinate with lightning speed, constantly updating targets as they gather new information.

Military Ground Vehicles

Traditional tanks are colossal vehicles. They carry heavy weapons to attack enemies and thick armor to protect the crew inside them. They are powered by huge, fuel-hungry engines and crawl across the land on big wheels or **endless tracks.**

These old behemoths are now being replaced by smaller, tougher **autonomous** tanks and carriers. These unmanned ground vehicles (UGV's) don't need a human crew, so they can be smaller and lighter. Without a crew they don't need as much space inside or such heavy armor, making them lighter and faster. That means they also use less fuel, often in short supply on battlefields.

Some robotic ground vehicles are configurable, so they can be used to carry supplies, mount weapons, or transport troops—and they can change jobs on the fly. They can also be fitted with cameras and sensors to patrol dangerous areas. Groups of autonomous tanks could also be used in combat.

An uncrewed supply vehicle can carry supplies, equipment, munitions, or injured troops. The THeMIS (*T*racked *H*ybrid *M*odular *I*nfantry *S*ystem) can be programmed to follow troops or navigate itself to a destination.

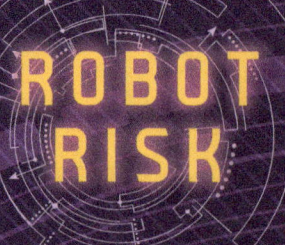

ROBOT RISK

Ethics of Military Robots

Is it right for robots to fight our wars for us? Some people argue that robot soldiers will keep people from being injured or killed. They would replace some soldiers and protect the rest by taking on the most dangerous duties. They might also be better at identifying and avoiding noncombatants, limiting innocent casualties.

But others argue that military robots are unethical. By taking the decision on whether to shoot away

Attack dog?
Many militaries use robot dogs to carry gear and scout terrain. But could they soon join in combat? In 2024, China showed off a robot dog mounted with a machine gun at military joint exercises in Cambodia. This renewed questions about military robots.

from people and preventing casualties in the military, robots might make war too "easy" for rich nations. An arms race could result in governments spending huge amounts of money on creating killer robots that they could have otherwise spent on helping their citizens.

If **autonomous** military robots are deployed, no one knows how they might be used. How will they value the safety of noncombatants? For example, if a robot predicts that it can kill 10 enemy fighters by firing a rocket, but that it might harm a civilian in doing so, will it be programmed to fire? If not, what will stop governments from overriding such programming?

Soldier 'bots
Someday, autonomous military robots might decide who to attack using **AI,** without any other human direction.

Bomb Disposal Units

Live bombs are extremely dangerous. To disable them safely, bomb disposal experts use remote-control robots. These bomb disposal units can deactivate explosives without putting anyone in harm's way. Such units usually have an arm, often with a high-powered water jet, to disable bombs. These remote-controlled devices have saved thousands of lives throughout the world.

Traditional bomb disposal units don't have much **autonomy.** They are usually operated remotely by a human at a safe distance. But because they save so many lives, some soldiers become attached to the bomb disposal unit with which they work. They may give their machine a name, keep track of its successful missions, or even hold a mock funeral if it is destroyed.

Newer bomb disposal units are being programmed with more autonomy, to enable them to locate and disable such common explosives as land mines.

Robot bomb squad
Bomb disposal robots usually have an arm with one or more end **effectors** to disable or safely set off explosive devices. Cameras help the control crew get a "robot's eye" view.

Robots in Disasters

In 2011, a powerful earthquake and **tsunami** struck the coast of Japan. The disaster knocked out power to the Fukushima Daiichi nuclear power plant, about 180 miles (290 kilometers) north of Tokyo. Because its electrically powered cooling system was disabled, nuclear fuel at the station's **reactors** melted through the steel containment structure and contaminated air and seawater. Tens of thousands of people were forced to leave their homes.

This tragedy led to a research revolution in disaster robotics. Japan was already a leading

An Atlas robot from the U.S.-based Institute for Human and Machine Cognition cuts a hole in a wall during the 2013 Robotics Challenge trials.

Clear the way! Japanese-based Team SCHAFT's S-One robot clears debris from its path during the 2013 Robotics Challenge trials.

country for robotics innovation, and many engineers turned their efforts to inventing robots to help in disasters and cleanup.

Fukushima also inspired the U.S. Defense Advanced Research Projects Agency (DARPA) to hold Robotics Challenges for rescue robots in 2013 and 2015. In 2017 they added a challenge for subterranean rescues, and in 2022 a new Triage Challenge to design robots to help rescuers identify victims in need of medical assistance.

HELLO, MY NAME IS:

Little Sunfish

Six years after the Fukushima disaster, scientists still had not located the radioactive core. Enter the Little Sunfish. The Fukushima Daiichi **nuclear reactors** had become a brutal training ground for disaster robots. **Radiation** fried their circuits. Steel and concrete walls interfered with radio signals. Unknown hazards lurked around every corner. But the Little Sunfish swam into the wrecked reactor cores to pinpoint where the melted fuel had gone. Now engineers are working to come up with ways to remove it. Nobody is sure exactly how this will be done, but it will involve robots.

AUTONOMY

LOW

Little Sunfish pulled a long cable behind it, which provided power and control. A human piloted it from a remote location.

SOME THANKS!

After finding the melted reactor fuel, the Little Sunfish had absorbed too much radiation to be around people. Workers sealed it in a steel container and buried it.

RADIATION EXPOSURE

Probably at least 200 **sieverts** per hour. Just a few sieverts total is enough to sicken or kill a person.

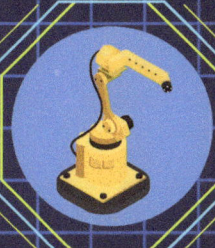

MAKER

The Japanese company Toshiba developed Little Sunfish.

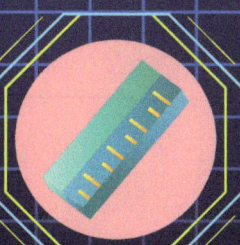

SIZE

4 ½ pounds (2 kilograms), 1 foot (30 centimeters) long

[25]

Types of Rescue Robots

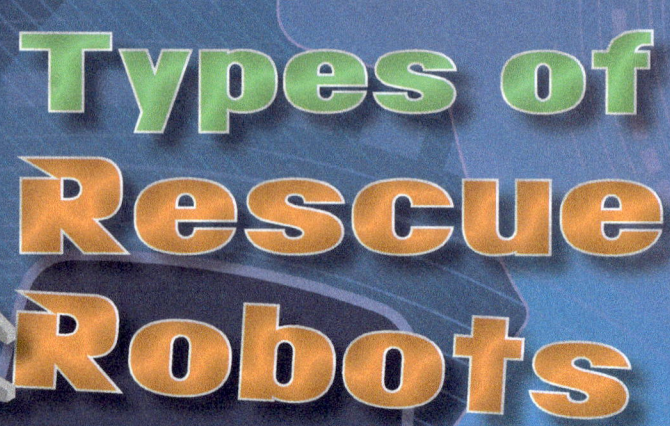

Robots designed for search and rescue come in a wide variety of shapes and sizes. Many designs have big, knobby tires or **endless tracks** along with bouncy suspension systems for moving over rough terrain.

Some robots designed for search and rescue missions look something like a snake. A long, thin body allows these tools to be maneuvered through the tight spaces of collapsed buildings to search for people.

A few search-and-rescue 'bots have legs. Atlas, one of the most advanced **humanoid** robots ever built, was originally designed for DARPA's Robotics Challenge. Other walking robots can have more than two legs for better stability. The robot that won the Robotics Challenge, called DRC-HUBO, has wheels attached to its knees and feet. When not performing tasks that required it to be at its full height, DRC-HUBO knelt down and rolled around.

Robots to the rescue

A snakebot (above) can slither into tight spaces to search for survivors. Other rescue robots have arms and legs to navigate in human-built surroundings. DRC-HUBO (left), the winner of the Robotics Challenge, has both legs and wheels.

HELLO, MY NAME IS:

Cyborg rescue cockroach

In future disasters, rescuers might work closely with the lowly cockroach! Cockroaches are very good at crawling through tight spaces. Some roboticists have built robots that mimic roaches. But others take a simpler approach. They are creating **cyborg** cockroaches from real insects. They attach wires to the antennae (feelers) and a computer chip to the bugs' backs. The cockroaches can be "steered" by small electric jolts to their antennae. The living bug does all the moving, so there's no need for motors, batteries, or metal legs. Cyborg cockroaches with tiny video and audio **sensors** could be used to locate survivors and scope out wreckage in disaster zones.

AUTONOMY

HIGH

Cyborg cockroaches behave in their usual ways unless they are given specific nudges by a human controller.

NO WAY TO TREAT A COCKROACH?

Some people think that modifying cockroaches—a living creature—in this way is wrong. But others think it's worth it if they can help save people.

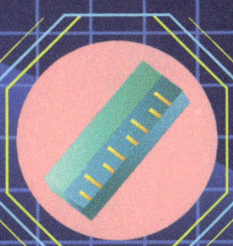

SIZE

Up to 5 inches (13 centimeters) long

MAKER

Mother Nature, plus some basic electronics

Firefighting Robots

Fires are another kind of dangerous situation where robots are lending a helping hand. Some robot firefighters look like small tanks. They roll in and shoot water or chemicals at fires. Flying **autonomous drones** can dump water from overhead. But whatever their shape, firefighting 'bots must be strong, tough—and waterproof.

Robotics engineers are working with fire and rescue departments to design the better robot helpers. Some are being programmed to understand spoken commands and hand gestures from firefighters. Robots equipped with thermal cameras and **AI** can patrol buildings and put out fires autonomously.

Colossal help
The Colossus fire-fighting robot helped extinguish the fire that badly damaged Notre Dame Cathedral in Paris, France, in 2019. Colossus is piloted remotely and can change shape to spray water, clear rubble, or carry victims to safety.

RoboCup Rescue Robot League

RoboCup is best known for hosting RoboCup Soccer, an international tournament for soccer-playing robots. But they also have a Rescue Robot League. High school and university teams worldwide design and program robots to quickly navigate difficult courses, perform tasks, and identify simulated victims. As technology and team skill improve, league officials create increasingly difficult courses. Robots must now operate **autonomously** through the course. Surprise obstacles may also be included. One year, league organizers covered the floor of one room with loose newspapers, stopping several robots in their tracks. Many team members have gone on to careers in robotics.

Tougher all the time
RoboCup rescue courses get more difficult each year, as technology and the skills of the teams improve.

Worldwide rescue
The RoboCup Rescue League hosts several events each year. All the events have standardized courses so that each robot's performance can be judged against that of hundreds of others from around the world.

Robots in Space Exploration

Robots are far better at exploring new places than humans are. They don't need air, water, or food. Just a power source will do. They can be designed to withstand a wide range of pressures, temperatures, and **radiation** levels.

We humans usually want to come back home when we're done exploring! A robot explorer can be left behind when its mission is over. For these reasons, robots have dominated space exploration. Humans have only made it as far as the moon, but **probes** and **rovers** explore the distant reaches of our solar system.

Government space agencies and even private companies are working to return people to the moon and send them to asteroids and Mars. But most space exploration will still be done with robots.

Mars explorers
The NASA rover Perseverance has been exploring the surface of Mars since 2021. Accompanying Perseverance is a small autonomous drone called Ingenuity, which in 2021 became the first machine to fly on another planet. Perseverence is the fifth rover to land on the Red Planet since 1976.

HELLO, MY NAME IS:

Canadarm2

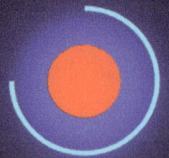

Canadarm2, one of Canada's contributions to the International Space Station (ISS), was launched in 2001. Today, it repairs and upgrades the station, catches incoming spacecraft, and even moves astronauts around! Grappling and berthing unpiloted supply vehicles is a tricky business. With input from astronauts on the ISS, ground crew on Earth, GPS data, and laser navigation systems, the Canadarm2 can grab the vehicles and guide them to airlocks. This precision operation has a "catchy" name: *cosmic catch*.

AUTONOMY
MEDIUM
Canadarm2 can be controlled autonomously or by astronauts.

LENGTH
56 feet (17 meters)

WEIGHT
3,300 pounds (1,500 kilograms) on Earth

MAKER
The Canadian company MacDonald, Dettwiler and Associates

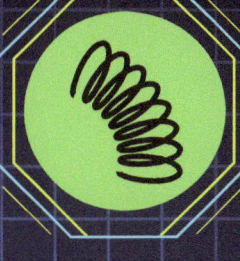

ROBOSLINKY
Canadarm2 doesn't have a fixed position. Each end of the arm can be "plugged in" to different slots around the space station exterior, allowing Canadarm2 to move like a giant Slinky. It also has a 50-foot (15-meter) boom attachment for observing remote parts of the ISS, as well as a handlike robotic attachment called Dextre.

Space Probes

Space **probes** orbit or fly past planets, moons, and asteroids, collecting data and sending them back to Earth. Probes usually contain few moving parts, but they need to be sturdy. First, a probe must survive the force of the rocket launch. Once it is in space, it needs to unfold and gather data. It has to be tough enough to withstand fast-moving space dust and rock

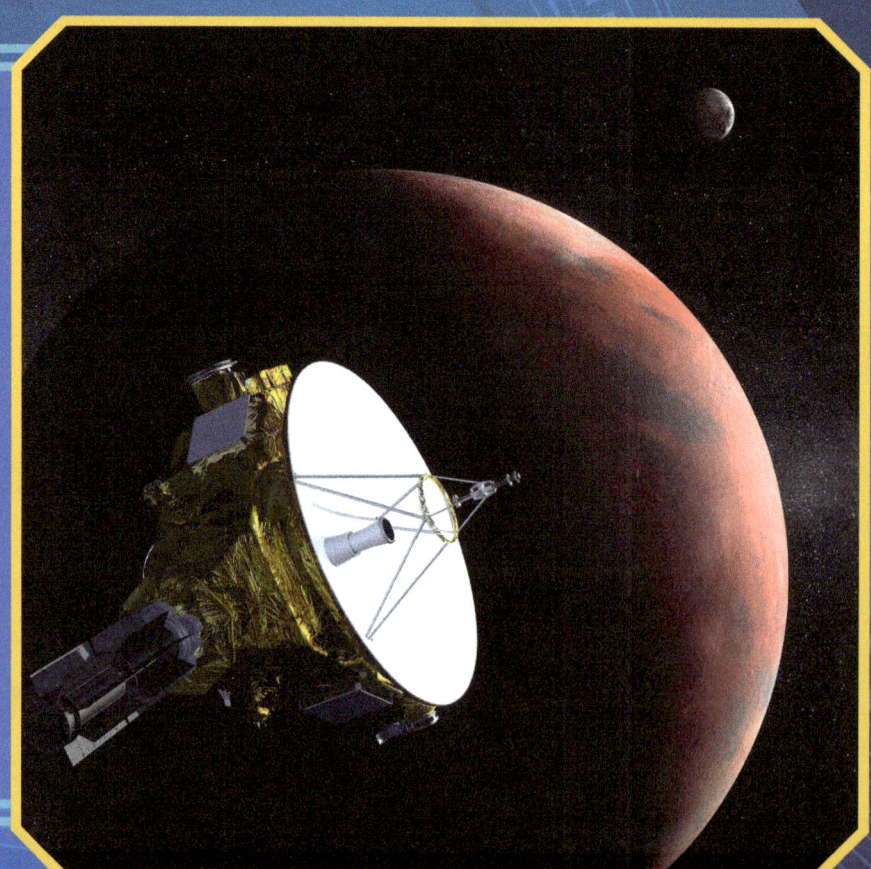

A long way from home
The probe New Horizons (shown in this artist's representation) has visited some of the most distant bodies in the solar system. Much of its work must be conducted **autonomously,** because commands from Earth take too long to reach it.

fragments hitting it as it travels. A probe must also be protected from strong **radiation** in space that can fry circuits. They must be able to fly autonomously, because signals from Earth can take hours to reach them. Most probes use thrusters and spinning discs called reaction wheels to maneuver in space. Probes have explored every planet and many other bodies in the solar system, and many more are planned.

Europa Clipper (shown in this illustration) will orbit Jupiter's icy moon Europa and study the salty oceans thought to exist under its frozen surface and check for signs of life.

[39]

Landers and Rovers

A lander is a spacecraft that lands on another body in space and collects data there. Simple landers work until their battery runs out of power. More complex landers have solar panels or even small nuclear-powered generators, which allow them to continue working for many months or even years.

A **rover** is a type of lander that can move around. Rovers are more complex than landers that remain in place, but they can provide information from different sites. Despite their complexity, well-built rovers can explore a planet or other body for a long time. The solar-powered rover Opportunity studied Mars for over 14 years, until its solar panels were covered by dust. What a resilient rover!

Rocks from the far side

In 2024, China's Chang'e 6 lander retrieved the first rock samples from the far side of the moon, the side that always faces away from Earth. A small capsule returned the samples to Earth for study. Chang'e 6 is China's sixth robotic lunar mission.

HELLO, MY NAME IS:

Perseverance

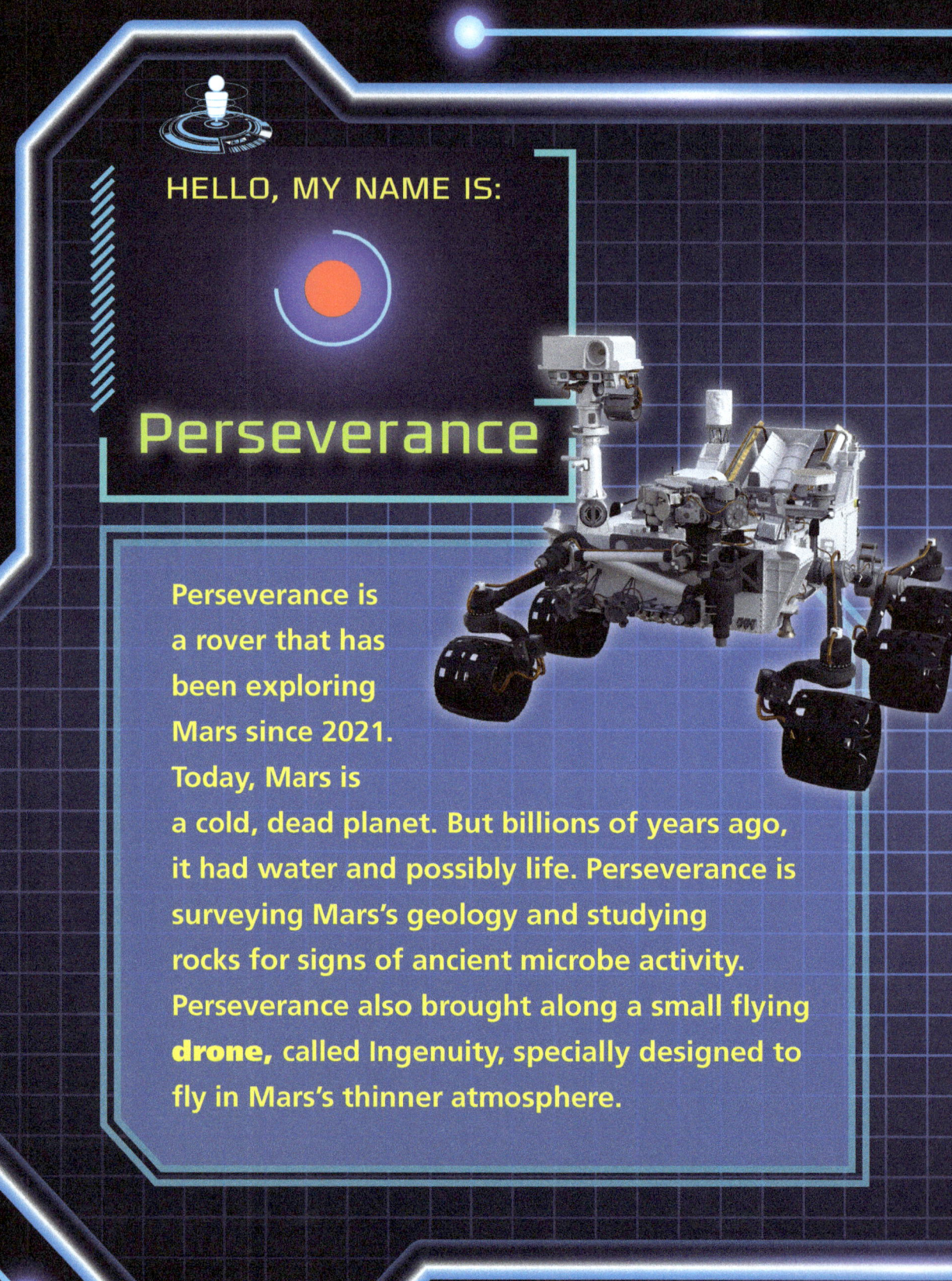

Perseverance is a rover that has been exploring Mars since 2021. Today, Mars is a cold, dead planet. But billions of years ago, it had water and possibly life. Perseverance is surveying Mars's geology and studying rocks for signs of ancient microbe activity. Perseverance also brought along a small flying **drone,** called Ingenuity, specially designed to fly in Mars's thinner atmosphere.

AUTONOMY

Medium

Perseverance receives lists of tasks and travel directions each day from Earth, but the rover drives autonomously and makes decisions about which routes to take to avoid hazards. It is also programmed to stop at interesting anomalies.

SIZE

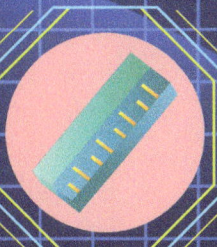

About the size of a car, weighing over 1 ton (1025 kilograms), the largest rover ever sent to another solar system body

POWER

Perseverance is powered by a small nuclear generator. The breakdown of radioactive materials produces its electricity.

TOOL KIT

Perseverance carries instruments for measuring weather and soil, drills, lasers, 23 cameras, and an onboard chemistry lab.

MAKER

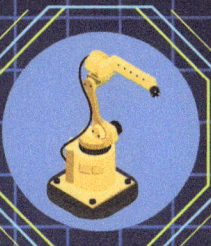

NASA's Jet Propulsion Laboratory (JPL) built Perseverance.

Ingenuity flying drone

Other Extreme Environments

Robots explore many places on Earth where it is dangerous or even impossible for people to go. In the 1990's, eight-legged robots named Dante and Dante II crept into volcanoes to taking samples and make measurements. Modern submersible robots explore deep ocean, venture under ice sheets, and dive into boiling volcanic vents, where divers can't go.

NASA and other space agencies have built **rovers** to explore scorching deserts or frozen lakes. These environments resemble what space robots might encounter on Mars or the icy moons of Jupiter and Saturn. Although these missions serve primarily to test rover ideas for future missions, they often discover things about their testing environments, too!

Dante's peak
Researchers used an eight-legged robot called Dante II to study Mount Spurr, a steep volcano in Alaska.

Hands-On Robotics

Want to get started making robots? Jump right in!

Robofest

Robofest is an international robot competition for students from 5th grade to college. Robots compete in eight categories, including BottleSumo (in which 'bots contend to knock either a bottle or each other out of the ring); RoboArts, for robots that make art with humans; and the Unknown Mission Challenge, in which the robot builders don't know what their robots will be asked to do until the actual competition. Their challenge is to build and program a robot that is ready for anything! There are also contests for robot vision and medical robots.

The contests are open-platform, meaning that robots can be built from any materials and programmed with any programming language. All robots must operate autonomously, with no human remote-control.

Robofest holds regional competitions in the United States and around the world. Regional champions gather for an annual final tournament at Lawrence Technological University in Southfield, Michigan.

Ready to rock?
Is this robot ready for anything? A young contender tests out his robot at Robofest in Bucharest, Romania, in 2022.

Weighty contender
This robot is competing in a Robofest robot weightlifting contest in 2024. The real challenge is lifting the barbell without falling over.

Also check out:
- RoboCup Rescue
- FIRST Robotics
- SeaPerch
- RoboGames

Or ask at your local school, library, or maker space.

Glossary

artificial intelligence (AI) the ability of a computer system to process information in a manner similar to human thought or to exhibit humanlike behavior.

automation the use of machines to perform tasks that require decision making.

autonomy the degree to which a robot can make decisions without input from a human operator to achieve a goal.

cyborg short for cybernetic organism, a living thing with computer or robotic modifications.

drone an uncrewed aerial vehicle. Most drones are piloted remotely, but some are autonomous.

effector the part of the robot's body, such as a wheel or a gripper, that is moved by an actuator and interacts with the environment to perform an action.

endless tracks a type of land vehicle propulsion system in which a long tread stretched between two or more wheels propels the vehicle.

humanoid shaped like or resembling a human.

nuclear reactor a device in which controlled nuclear fission reactions take place, usually for the production of electricity.

probe an uncrewed space vehicle that orbits a space body to collect data.

radiation energy given off in the form of waves or tiny particles of matter. Radiation given off from nuclear reactors and that found in space can harm people and damage electronics.

rover a vehicle that moves around on the surface of a moon or planet to collect scientific samples and data.

sievert a unit of radiation exposure.

sensor a device that takes in information from the outside world and translates it into code.

tsunami a series of powerful ocean waves produced by an earthquake, landslide, volcanic eruption, or asteroid impact. Tsunami waves can travel great distances and still retain much of their strength.

Index

A
arms race, 19
artificial intelligence (AI), 6, 19
automation, 6, 8
autonomy, 4; disaster robot, 25, 28, 30, 32; military robot, 6-21; space robot, 37, 38, 43

B
bomb disposal units, 4, 9, 20-21

C
Chang'e 6 (lander), 41
Canadarm2 (robot), 36-37
cockroaches, cyborg rescue, 28-29
Colossus (robot), 313

D
Dante and Dante II (robots), 44-45
Defense Advanced Research Projects Agency (DARPA), 23, 26
disaster robots, 4-5, 22-33
DRC-HUBO (robot), 26-27
drones, 4, 10-15, 28

E
Earth exploration, 44-45
effectors, 21
endless tracks, 26
ethical issues, 8, 18-19, 29
Europe Clipper (probe), 39

F
firefighting robots, 30-31
Fukushima Daiichi nuclear power plant, 22-25

G
guided missiles, 6-7

H
human-in-the-loop systems, 8-9
human-on-the-loop systems, 8
humanoid robots, 7, 26-27

I
Ingenuity (drone), 34-35, 42-43
International Space Station (ISS), 36-37

J
Japan earthquake and tsunami, 22-25, 32
Jupiter, 39, 44

L
landers, 40
Little Sunfish (robot), 24-25

M
Magura V5 (sea drone), 7
Mars, 34-35, 40-44
military robots, 6-21. *See also* bomb disposal units; drones; tanks
moon, 34
Mount Spurr, 44-45
MQ-9 Reaper (drone), 12-13, 16

N
National Aeronautics and Space Administration (NASA), 42-45
New Horizons probe, 38
Notre Dame Cathedral, 31
nuclear reactors, 22, 24-25

P
Perseverance (rover), 34-35, 42-43

R
radiation, 24, 25, 34, 39
rescue robots, 26-29, 32-33
RoboCup Rescue Robot League, 32-33
Robofest (competition), 46-47
robot dogs, 18
Robotics Challenges, 22, 23, 26-27
rovers, 34-35, 40-44

S
snakebots, 26-27
space exploration, 4-5, 34-43
space probes, 38-39
swarming aircraft, 14-15

T
tanks, 7, 16-17
telepresence robots, 21
THeMIS, 17
Toshiba (company), 25

U
uncrewed aerial vehicles. *See* drones
uncrewed ground vehicles (UGV's), 16

V
Valkyrie (drone), 14
volcanoes, 44-45

www.ingramcontent.com/pod-product-compliance
Lightning Source LLC
Chambersburg PA
CBHW061254170426
43191CB00041B/2425